I0558987

· - - - - - · Dedication · - - - - - ·

With love for Marisa and Whitney

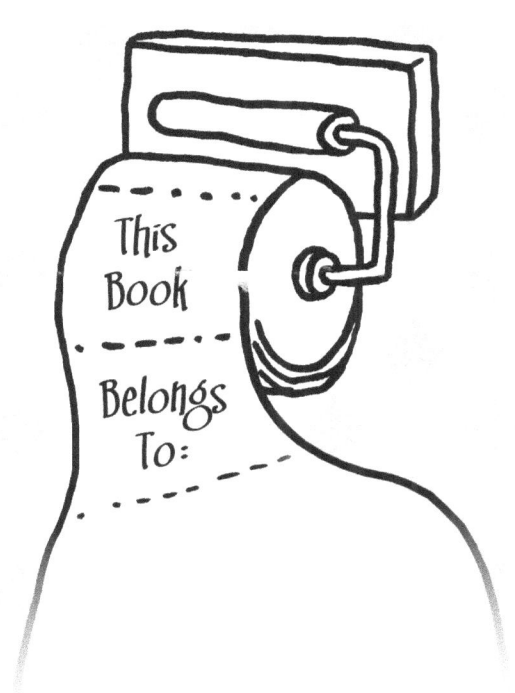

This Book Belongs To:

THE DOODY STORY

OR POTTY ECOLOGY

Marc Leeds

Illustrated by
Eileen Leeds

Charles Bruce Foundation
Carlisle, Pennsylvania

A short while ago, in a house not far away, a small blonde girl had a problem. She did not like sitting on the potty seat in the bathroom all alone.

The potty seat was okay, as far as potty seats go. It had a music box that sat on top of the big white toilet. The music box played *How Dry I Am* when her mother switched it on, but the small blonde girl wanted company, not music.

One day she figured out how to get some company. The small blonde girl knew that her parents always tried very hard to answer all her questions.

Her daddy was especially patient with even her silliest questions. That's because he never thought her questions were silly.

So one Saturday morning while her mom slept late, the small blonde girl went to her daddy and asked him to follow her.

She led him by the hand into her bathroom and sat him down on the big red stool she used to reach the sink. She climbed her way up to the potty seat, brushed her bangs from her eyes, and asked, "Daddy, where do the doodies go?"

"Where do the doodies go?"
he seemed to ask right back at her.

"No fair, Daddy," she giggled.

"I asked you first!
Where do they go after
we flush the toilet?"

Her daddy sat thinking for a moment. His eyes lit up, his mouth widened into a smile and he said, "You want to know where the doodies go? Well, I'll tell you."

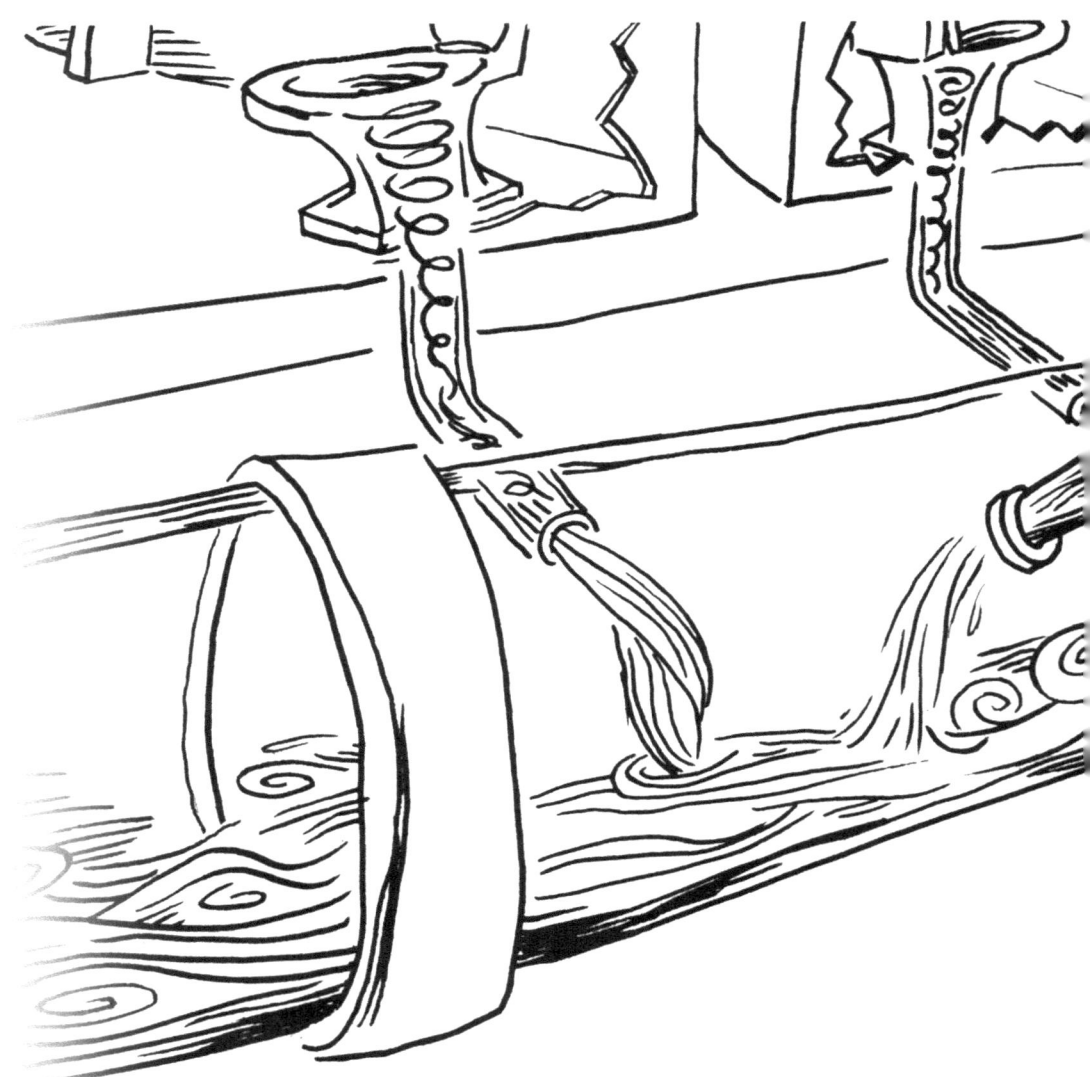

"When the doodies get flushed, they go spinning, spinning, spinning down the toilet and into the pipes running through the basement."

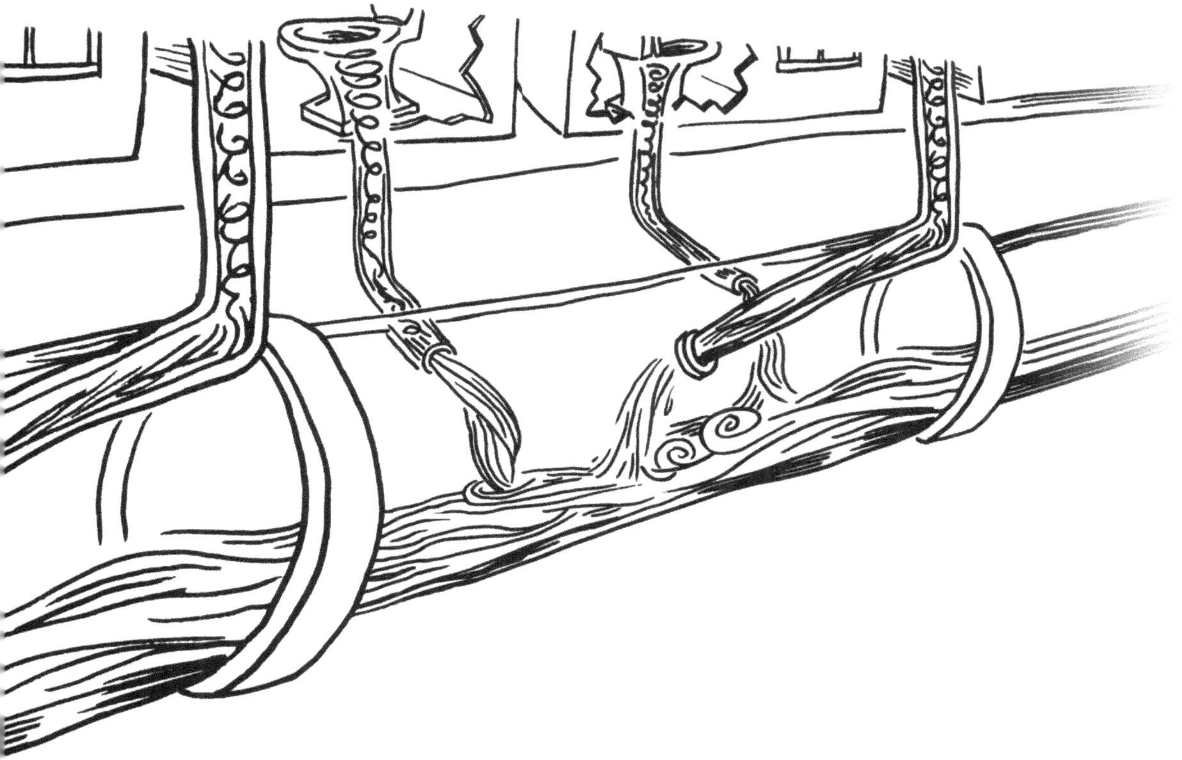

"Down the pipes, out to the sewers beneath the streets, where they rush along until they get to the sewage treatment plant."

"What's that, daddy?"

"I was just about to tell you,
but that is a very good question.
That's where all the doodies from
all over go into big tanks. They get
mushed together in a huge mixing
machine, much bigger than our food
blender in the kitchen, and the
workers pour in lots of chemicals
to clean up all the harmful
stuff in them."

"Then when the doodies are clean, they get pumped out through more pipes until they reach the rivers. The rivers carry them out to the ocean where they fall to the bottom of the sea.

"The cleaned up mush mixes with the sand at the bottom of the ocean and helps feed the plants that grow there."

"Tiny fish come along and eat the little plants. Then some bigger fish come along and eat the tiny fish. Then larger fish come and eat those fish. Then comes the great tuna fish who eats the other fish."

"And then out in his fishing boat, comes the . . ."

"FISHERMAN!" squealed the small blonde girl.

"That's right! The fisherman grabs the tuna in his giant nets and brings him on board. Then he steers his boat back to the docks where he sells the tuna to the tuna fish factory."

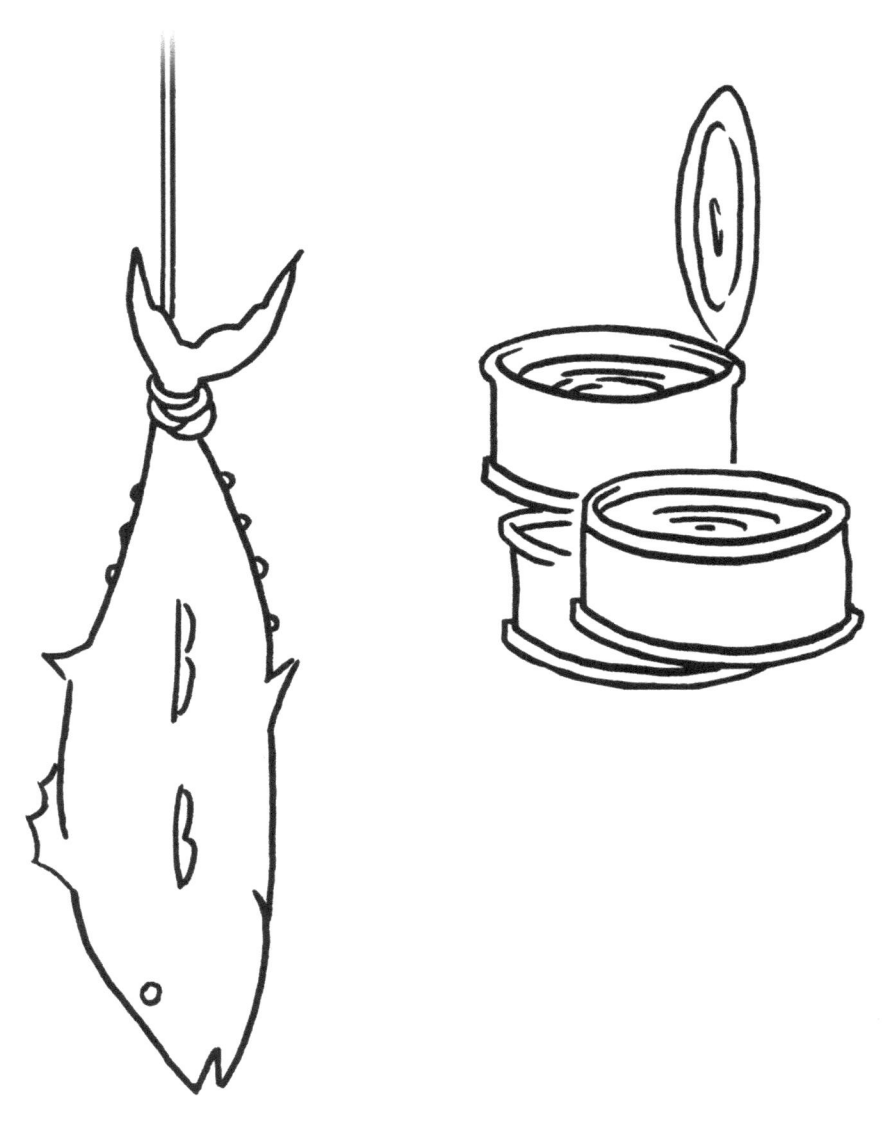

"What happens there, daddy?"

"The tuna is cut into small circles of meat and placed in cans. The cans are packed into boxes. The boxes are packed into crates. The crates are loaded onto trucks. And the trucks deliver the cans of tuna fish to the…"

"GROCERY STORE!" cried the small blonde girl.

"That's right! And then the mommies and the daddies bring their children to the store to shop for food. That's when they buy some cans of tuna fish, mayonnaise, lemon juice, lettuce, tomatoes and bread."

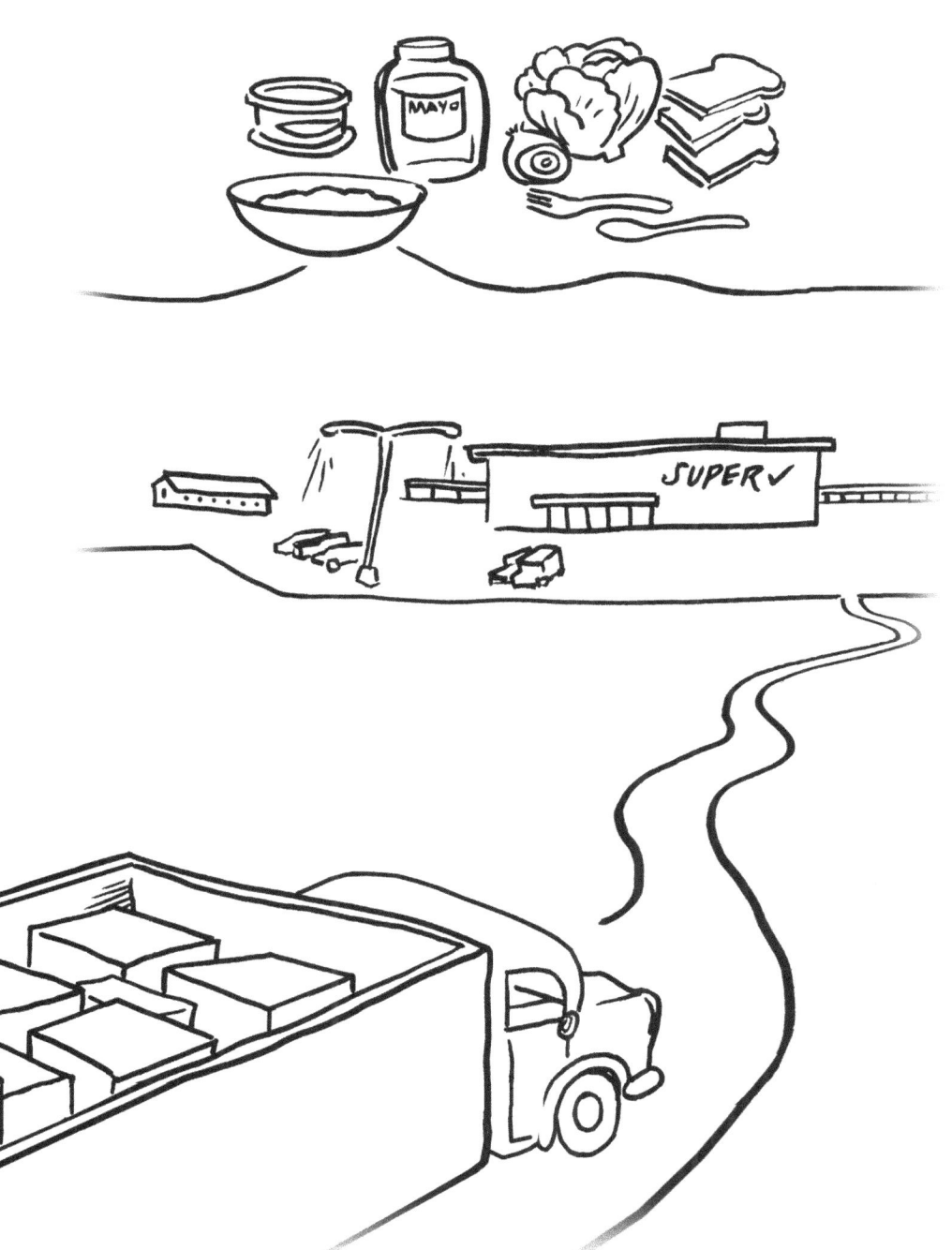

"They go home to make some sandwiches, and you know what happens then?"

"Oh, Daddy, can I guess?" asked the small blonde girl.

"After they eat they have to go to the bathroom."

"How did you get so smart?" her daddy asked with a big smile.

"And then," the small blonde girl jumped in to say, "when the doodies get flushed, they go spinning, spinning, spinning down the toilet and into the pipes running through the basement."

"Right again," said her dad. "And then it starts all over again."

"Tell it again, daddy! Tell it again!"

"I'll tell you the story the next time you have to go to the bathroom. Okay?"

The small blonde girl thought for a moment and said, "Sure, and that way you could keep me company."

Years passed, and many tellings of the doody story passed as well.

The small blonde girl wanted to hear the story as often as possible. Sometimes, she even wanted to hear it as a bedtime story.

Then the small blonde girl had a younger sister, also blonde, who was ready for potty training. And as their parents laid awake in bed early one Saturday morning, they could hear their daughters shuffle down the hall to the bathroom.

The small blonde girl, who was now the big sister, lifted her little sister up to the potty seat. She kneeled on the big red stool and told her, "It's time you knew where all the doodies go."

"When the doodies get flushed, they go spinning, spinning, spinning down the toilet and into the pipes running through the basement. Just a second.

"Hey, dad!" she called down the hall. "Come in and help me tell the story."

"I'll be right there," he called to the girls.

He turned to his wife and said, "I have to go now..."

Duty Calls!

The End!

In his spare time away
from raising babies into
useful and caring adults,
Marc Leeds authored
The Vonnegut Encyclopedia.

Learn more about
Eileen Leeds'
artwork at lileen.com